HAL•LEONARD
INSTRUMENTAL
PLAY-ALONG

VIOLIN

Disney CLASSICS

To access audio, visit:
www.halleonard.com/mylibrary

7418-5613-2686-7820

The following songs are the property of:

BOURNE CO.
Music Publishers
5 West 37th Street
New York, NY 10018

Baby Mine
Give a Little Whistle
Heigh-Ho
I've Got No Strings

Some Day My Prince Will Come
When You Wish Upon a Star
Whistle While You Work
Who's Afraid of the Big Bad Wolf?

Disney characters and artwork © Disney Enterprises, Inc.

ISBN 978-1-4584-1603-2

HAL•LEONARD®
Visit Hal Leonard Online at **www.halleonard.com**

World headquarters, contact:
Hal Leonard
7777 West Bluemound Road
Milwaukee, WI 53213
Email: info@halleonard.com

In Europe, contact:
Hal Leonard Europe Limited
Dettingen Way
Bury St. Edmunds, Suffolk, IP33 3YB
Email: info@halleonardeurope.com

In Australia, contact:
Hal Leonard Australia Pty. Ltd.
4 Lentara Court
Cheltenham, Victoria, 3192 Australia
Email: info@halleonard.com.au

ALICE IN WONDERLAND

from Walt Disney's ALICE IN WONDERLAND

Words by BOB HILLIARD
Music by SAMMY FAIN

VIOLIN

BABY MINE

from Walt Disney's DUMBO

VIOLIN

Words by NED WASHINGTON
Music by FRANK CHURCHILL

BELLA NOTTE

(This Is the Night)

from Walt Disney's LADY AND THE TRAMP

Words and Music by PEGGY LEE
and SONNY BURKE

Violin

GIVE A LITTLE WHISTLE

from Walt Disney's PINOCCHIO

VIOLIN

Words by NED WASHINGTON
Music by LEIGH HARLINE

HEIGH-HO

The Dwarfs' Marching Song from Walt Disney's SNOW WHITE AND THE SEVEN DWARFS

Violin

Words by LARRY MOREY
Music by FRANK CHURCHILL

I'VE GOT NO STRINGS

from Walt Disney's PINOCCHIO

VIOLIN

Words by NED WASHINGTON
Music by LEIGH HARLINE

LITTLE APRIL SHOWER

from Walt Disney's BAMBI

Words by Larry Morey
Music by FRANK CHURCHILL

ONCE UPON A DREAM

from Walt Disney's SLEEPING BEAUTY

Violin

Words and Music by SAMMY FAIN
and JACK LAWRENCE
Adapted from a Theme by Tchaikovsky

SOME DAY MY PRINCE WILL COME

from Walt Disney's SNOW WHITE AND THE SEVEN DWARFS

VIOLIN

Words by LARRY MOREY
Music by FRANK CHURCHILL

THE UNBIRTHDAY SONG

from Walt Disney's ALICE IN WONDERLAND

VIOLIN

Words and Music by MACK DAVID,
AL HOFFMAN and JERRY LIVINGSTON

WHEN YOU WISH UPON A STAR

from Walt Disney's PINOCCHIO

Words by NED WASHINGTON
Music by LEIGH HARLINE

VIOLIN

WHISTLE WHILE YOU WORK

from Walt Disney's SNOW WHITE AND THE SEVEN DWARFS

VIOLIN

Words by LARRY MOREY
Music by FRANK CHURCHILL

WHO'S AFRAID OF THE BIG BAD WOLF?

from Walt Disney's THREE LITTLE PIGS

VIOLIN

Words and Music by FRANK CHURCHILL
Additional Lyric by ANN RONELL

YOU CAN FLY! YOU CAN FLY! YOU CAN FLY!

from Walt Disney's PETER PAN

Words by SAMMY CAHN
Music by SAMMY FAIN

VIOLIN